The Effective Meeting Agenda
AgendaMeetingbooks1

Copyright: Published in the United States by Rita L. Spears

Published April 2017

All rights reserved. No part of this publication may be reproduced, stored in retrieval system, copied in any form or by any means, electronic, mechanical, photocopying, recording or otherwise transmitted without written permission from the publisher. Please do not participate in or encourage piracy of this material in any way. You must not circulate this book in any format. Rita L. Spears *does not control or direct users' actions and is not responsible for the information or content shared, harm and/or actions of the book readers.*

ISBN-13: 978-1545541630

ISBN-10: 1545541639

MEETING MINUTES TEMPLATE

Meeting Date:	
Meeting Time:	
Meeting Location:	
Meeting Called By:	Designation:
Meeting Purpose:	
Note Taker:	
Timekeeper:	

AGENDA TOPICS

[Write topic here]	[Presenter]
[Add another topic if any]	[Presenter]

Important Discussion Points
1.   4.
2.   5.
3.   6.

Conclusion

Action items	[Presenter]
[Topic here]	[Name]
[Topic here]	[Name]

Any notes

MEETING MINUTES TEMPLATE

Meeting Date:	
Meeting Time:	
Meeting Location:	
Meeting Called By: Designation:	
Meeting Purpose:	
Note Taker:	
Timekeeper:	

AGENDA TOPICS

[Write topic here]	[Presenter]
[Add another topic if any]	[Presenter]

Important Discussion Points	
1.	4.
2.	5.
3.	6.

Conclusion

Action items	[Presenter]
[Topic here]	[Name]
[Topic here]	[Name]
Any notes	

MEETING MINUTES TEMPLATE

Meeting Date:	
Meeting Time:	
Meeting Location:	
Meeting Called By:　　　Designation:	
Meeting Purpose:	
Note Taker:	
Timekeeper:	

AGENDA TOPICS

[Write topic here]	[Presenter]
[Add another topic if any]	[Presenter]

Important Discussion Points

1.　　　　　　　4.
2.　　　　　　　5.
3.　　　　　　　6.

Conclusion

Action items	[Presenter]
[Topic here]	[Name]
[Topic here]	[Name]
Any notes	

MEETING MINUTES TEMPLATE

Meeting Date:	
Meeting Time:	
Meeting Location:	
Meeting Called By:	Designation:
Meeting Purpose:	
Note Taker:	
Timekeeper:	

AGENDA TOPICS

[Write topic here]	[Presenter]
[Add another topic if any]	[Presenter]

Important Discussion Points
1.   4.
2.   5.
3.   6.

Conclusion

Action items	[Presenter]
[Topic here]	[Name]
[Topic here]	[Name]

Any notes

MEETING MINUTES TEMPLATE

Meeting Date:	
Meeting Time:	
Meeting Location:	
Meeting Called By: Designation:	
Meeting Purpose:	
Note Taker:	
Timekeeper:	

AGENDA TOPICS

[Write topic here]	[Presenter]
[Add another topic if any]	[Presenter]

Important Discussion Points

1.   4.
2.   5.
3.   6.

Conclusion

Action items	[Presenter]
[Topic here]	[Name]
[Topic here]	[Name]

Any notes

MEETING MINUTES TEMPLATE

Meeting Date:	
Meeting Time:	
Meeting Location:	
Meeting Called By: Designation:	
Meeting Purpose:	
Note Taker:	
Timekeeper:	

AGENDA TOPICS

[Write topic here]	[Presenter]
[Add another topic if any]	[Presenter]

Important Discussion Points	
1.	4.
2.	5.
3.	6.

Conclusion

Action items	[Presenter]
[Topic here]	[Name]
[Topic here]	[Name]
Any notes	

MEETING MINUTES TEMPLATE

Meeting Date:	
Meeting Time:	
Meeting Location:	
Meeting Called By:	Designation:
Meeting Purpose:	
Note Taker:	
Timekeeper:	

AGENDA TOPICS

[Write topic here]	[Presenter]
[Add another topic if any]	[Presenter]

Important Discussion Points
1.   4.
2.   5.
3.   6.

Conclusion

Action items	[Presenter]
[Topic here]	[Name]
[Topic here]	[Name]
Any notes	

MEETING MINUTES TEMPLATE

Meeting Date:	
Meeting Time:	
Meeting Location:	
Meeting Called By:	Designation:
Meeting Purpose:	
Note Taker:	
Timekeeper:	

AGENDA TOPICS

[Write topic here]	[Presenter]
[Add another topic if any]	[Presenter]

Important Discussion Points
1.   4.
2.   5.
3.   6.

Conclusion

Action items	[Presenter]
[Topic here]	[Name]
[Topic here]	[Name]

Any notes

MEETING MINUTES TEMPLATE

Meeting Date:
Meeting Time:
Meeting Location:
Meeting Called By: Designation:
Meeting Purpose:
Note Taker:
Timekeeper:

AGENDA TOPICS

[Write topic here]	[Presenter]
[Add another topic if any]	[Presenter]

Important Discussion Points

1.   4.
2.   5.
3.   6.

Conclusion

Action items	[Presenter]
[Topic here]	[Name]
[Topic here]	[Name]
Any notes	

MEETING MINUTES TEMPLATE

Meeting Date:	
Meeting Time:	
Meeting Location:	
Meeting Called By:	Designation:
Meeting Purpose:	
Note Taker:	
Timekeeper:	

AGENDA TOPICS

[Write topic here]	[Presenter]
[Add another topic if any]	[Presenter]

Important Discussion Points
1.   4.
2.   5.
3.   6.

Conclusion

Action items	[Presenter]
[Topic here]	[Name]
[Topic here]	[Name]

Any notes

MEETING MINUTES TEMPLATE

Meeting Date:	
Meeting Time:	
Meeting Location:	
Meeting Called By:	Designation:
Meeting Purpose:	
Note Taker:	
Timekeeper:	

AGENDA TOPICS

[Write topic here]	[Presenter]
[Add another topic if any]	[Presenter]

Important Discussion Points
1.   4.
2.   5.
3.   6.

Conclusion

Action items	[Presenter]
[Topic here]	[Name]
[Topic here]	[Name]

Any notes

MEETING MINUTES TEMPLATE

Meeting Date:	
Meeting Time:	
Meeting Location:	
Meeting Called By:	Designation:
Meeting Purpose:	
Note Taker:	
Timekeeper:	

AGENDA TOPICS

[Write topic here]	[Presenter]
[Add another topic if any]	[Presenter]

Important Discussion Points

1.   4.
2.   5.
3.   6.

Conclusion

Action items	[Presenter]
[Topic here]	[Name]
[Topic here]	[Name]

Any notes

MEETING MINUTES TEMPLATE

Meeting Date:	
Meeting Time:	
Meeting Location:	
Meeting Called By: Designation:	
Meeting Purpose:	
Note Taker:	
Timekeeper:	

AGENDA TOPICS

[Write topic here]	[Presenter]
[Add another topic if any]	[Presenter]

Important Discussion Points
1.   4.
2.   5.
3.   6.

Conclusion

Action items	[Presenter]
[Topic here]	[Name]
[Topic here]	[Name]

Any notes

MEETING MINUTES TEMPLATE

Meeting Date:	
Meeting Time:	
Meeting Location:	
Meeting Called By:	Designation:
Meeting Purpose:	
Note Taker:	
Timekeeper:	

AGENDA TOPICS

[Write topic here]	[Presenter]
[Add another topic if any]	[Presenter]

Important Discussion Points
1.   4.
2.   5.
3.   6.

Conclusion

Action items	[Presenter]
[Topic here]	[Name]
[Topic here]	[Name]

Any notes

MEETING MINUTES TEMPLATE

Meeting Date:	
Meeting Time:	
Meeting Location:	
Meeting Called By:	Designation:
Meeting Purpose:	
Note Taker:	
Timekeeper:	

AGENDA TOPICS

[Write topic here]	[Presenter]
[Add another topic if any]	[Presenter]

Important Discussion Points
1.   4.
2.   5.
3.   6.

Conclusion

Action items	[Presenter]
[Topic here]	[Name]
[Topic here]	[Name]
Any notes	

MEETING MINUTES TEMPLATE

Meeting Date:	
Meeting Time:	
Meeting Location:	
Meeting Called By: Designation:	
Meeting Purpose:	
Note Taker:	
Timekeeper:	

AGENDA TOPICS

[Write topic here]	[Presenter]
[Add another topic if any]	[Presenter]

Important Discussion Points
1.   4.
2.   5.
3.   6.

Conclusion

Action items	[Presenter]
[Topic here]	[Name]
[Topic here]	[Name]
Any notes	

MEETING MINUTES TEMPLATE

Meeting Date:	
Meeting Time:	
Meeting Location:	
Meeting Called By:	Designation:
Meeting Purpose:	
Note Taker:	
Timekeeper:	

AGENDA TOPICS

[Write topic here]	[Presenter]
[Add another topic if any]	[Presenter]

Important Discussion Points
1.   4.
2.   5.
3.   6.

Conclusion

Action items	[Presenter]
[Topic here]	[Name]
[Topic here]	[Name]
Any notes	

MEETING MINUTES TEMPLATE

Meeting Date:	
Meeting Time:	
Meeting Location:	
Meeting Called By: Designation:	
Meeting Purpose:	
Note Taker:	
Timekeeper:	

AGENDA TOPICS

[Write topic here]	[Presenter]
[Add another topic if any]	[Presenter]

Important Discussion Points
1. 4.
2. 5.
3. 6.

Conclusion

Action items	[Presenter]
[Topic here]	[Name]
[Topic here]	[Name]
Any notes	

MEETING MINUTES TEMPLATE

Meeting Date:	
Meeting Time:	
Meeting Location:	
Meeting Called By:	Designation:
Meeting Purpose:	
Note Taker:	
Timekeeper:	

AGENDA TOPICS

[Write topic here]	[Presenter]
[Add another topic if any]	[Presenter]

Important Discussion Points
1.   4.
2.   5.
3.   6.

Conclusion

Action items	[Presenter]
[Topic here]	[Name]
[Topic here]	[Name]
Any notes	

MEETING MINUTES TEMPLATE

Meeting Date:	
Meeting Time:	
Meeting Location:	
Meeting Called By: Designation:	
Meeting Purpose:	
Note Taker:	
Timekeeper:	

AGENDA TOPICS

[Write topic here]	[Presenter]
[Add another topic if any]	[Presenter]

Important Discussion Points
1.   4.
2.   5.
3.   6.

Conclusion

Action items	[Presenter]
[Topic here]	[Name]
[Topic here]	[Name]
Any notes	

MEETING MINUTES TEMPLATE

Meeting Date:	
Meeting Time:	
Meeting Location:	
Meeting Called By: Designation:	
Meeting Purpose:	
Note Taker:	
Timekeeper:	

AGENDA TOPICS

[Write topic here]	[Presenter]
[Add another topic if any]	[Presenter]

Important Discussion Points
1.   4.
2.   5.
3.   6.

Conclusion

Action items	[Presenter]
[Topic here]	[Name]
[Topic here]	[Name]
Any notes	

MEETING MINUTES TEMPLATE

Meeting Date:	
Meeting Time:	
Meeting Location:	
Meeting Called By:	Designation:
Meeting Purpose:	
Note Taker:	
Timekeeper:	

AGENDA TOPICS

[Write topic here]	[Presenter]
[Add another topic if any]	[Presenter]

Important Discussion Points

1.   4.
2.   5.
3.   6.

Conclusion

Action items	[Presenter]
[Topic here]	[Name]
[Topic here]	[Name]

Any notes

MEETING MINUTES TEMPLATE

Meeting Date:	
Meeting Time:	
Meeting Location:	
Meeting Called By:　　　Designation:	
Meeting Purpose:	
Note Taker:	
Timekeeper:	

AGENDA TOPICS

[Write topic here]	[Presenter]
[Add another topic if any]	[Presenter]

Important Discussion Points
1.　　　　　　　4.
2.　　　　　　　5.
3.　　　　　　　6.

Conclusion

Action items	[Presenter]
[Topic here]	[Name]
[Topic here]	[Name]
Any notes	

MEETING MINUTES TEMPLATE

Meeting Date:	
Meeting Time:	
Meeting Location:	
Meeting Called By: Designation:	
Meeting Purpose:	
Note Taker:	
Timekeeper:	

AGENDA TOPICS

[Write topic here]	[Presenter]
[Add another topic if any]	[Presenter]

Important Discussion Points
1.   4.
2.   5.
3.   6.

Conclusion

Action items	[Presenter]
[Topic here]	[Name]
[Topic here]	[Name]
Any notes	

MEETING MINUTES TEMPLATE

Meeting Date:	
Meeting Time:	
Meeting Location:	
Meeting Called By:	Designation:
Meeting Purpose:	
Note Taker:	
Timekeeper:	

AGENDA TOPICS

[Write topic here]	[Presenter]
[Add another topic if any]	[Presenter]

Important Discussion Points
1.   4.
2.   5.
3.   6.

Conclusion

Action items	[Presenter]
[Topic here]	[Name]
[Topic here]	[Name]

Any notes

MEETING MINUTES TEMPLATE

Meeting Date:
Meeting Time:
Meeting Location:
Meeting Called By: Designation:
Meeting Purpose:
Note Taker:
Timekeeper:

AGENDA TOPICS

[Write topic here]	[Presenter]
[Add another topic if any]	[Presenter]

Important Discussion Points
1.   4.
2.   5.
3.   6.

Conclusion

Action items	[Presenter]
[Topic here]	[Name]
[Topic here]	[Name]
Any notes	

MEETING MINUTES TEMPLATE

Meeting Date:	
Meeting Time:	
Meeting Location:	
Meeting Called By: Designation:	
Meeting Purpose:	
Note Taker:	
Timekeeper:	

AGENDA TOPICS

[Write topic here]	[Presenter]
[Add another topic if any]	[Presenter]

Important Discussion Points
1. 4.
2. 5.
3. 6.

Conclusion

Action items	[Presenter]
[Topic here]	[Name]
[Topic here]	[Name]
Any notes	

MEETING MINUTES TEMPLATE

Meeting Date:	
Meeting Time:	
Meeting Location:	
Meeting Called By:	Designation:
Meeting Purpose:	
Note Taker:	
Timekeeper:	

AGENDA TOPICS

[Write topic here]	[Presenter]
[Add another topic if any]	[Presenter]

Important Discussion Points

1.   4.
2.   5.
3.   6.

Conclusion

Action items	[Presenter]
[Topic here]	[Name]
[Topic here]	[Name]

Any notes

MEETING MINUTES TEMPLATE

Meeting Date:	
Meeting Time:	
Meeting Location:	
Meeting Called By:	Designation:
Meeting Purpose:	
Note Taker:	
Timekeeper:	
AGENDA TOPICS	
[Write topic here]	[Presenter]
[Add another topic if any]	[Presenter]
Important Discussion Points 1. 4. 2. 5. 3. 6.	
Conclusion	
Action items	[Presenter]
[Topic here]	[Name]
[Topic here]	[Name]
Any notes	

MEETING MINUTES TEMPLATE

Meeting Date:	
Meeting Time:	
Meeting Location:	
Meeting Called By:	Designation:
Meeting Purpose:	
Note Taker:	
Timekeeper:	

AGENDA TOPICS

[Write topic here]	[Presenter]
[Add another topic if any]	[Presenter]

Important Discussion Points
1.   4.
2.   5.
3.   6.

Conclusion

Action items	[Presenter]
[Topic here]	[Name]
[Topic here]	[Name]

Any notes

MEETING MINUTES TEMPLATE

Meeting Date:	
Meeting Time:	
Meeting Location:	
Meeting Called By:	Designation:
Meeting Purpose:	
Note Taker:	
Timekeeper:	

AGENDA TOPICS

[Write topic here]	[Presenter]
[Add another topic if any]	[Presenter]

Important Discussion Points
1. 4.
2. 5.
3. 6.

Conclusion

Action items	[Presenter]
[Topic here]	[Name]
[Topic here]	[Name]

Any notes

MEETING MINUTES TEMPLATE

Meeting Date:	
Meeting Time:	
Meeting Location:	
Meeting Called By:	Designation:
Meeting Purpose:	
Note Taker:	
Timekeeper:	

AGENDA TOPICS

[Write topic here]	[Presenter]
[Add another topic if any]	[Presenter]

Important Discussion Points
1.   4.
2.   5.
3.   6.

Conclusion

Action items	[Presenter]
[Topic here]	[Name]
[Topic here]	[Name]
Any notes	

MEETING MINUTES TEMPLATE

Meeting Date:	
Meeting Time:	
Meeting Location:	
Meeting Called By:　　　　Designation:	
Meeting Purpose:	
Note Taker:	
Timekeeper:	

AGENDA TOPICS

[Write topic here]	[Presenter]
[Add another topic if any]	[Presenter]

Important Discussion Points
1.　　　　　　4.
2.　　　　　　5.
3.　　　　　　6.

Conclusion

Action items	[Presenter]
[Topic here]	[Name]
[Topic here]	[Name]
Any notes	

MEETING MINUTES TEMPLATE

Meeting Date:	
Meeting Time:	
Meeting Location:	
Meeting Called By:	Designation:
Meeting Purpose:	
Note Taker:	
Timekeeper:	

AGENDA TOPICS

[Write topic here]	[Presenter]
[Add another topic if any]	[Presenter]

Important Discussion Points
1.   4.
2.   5.
3.   6.

Conclusion

Action items	[Presenter]
[Topic here]	[Name]
[Topic here]	[Name]

Any notes

MEETING MINUTES TEMPLATE

Meeting Date:	
Meeting Time:	
Meeting Location:	
Meeting Called By:	Designation:
Meeting Purpose:	
Note Taker:	
Timekeeper:	

AGENDA TOPICS

[Write topic here]	[Presenter]
[Add another topic if any]	[Presenter]

Important Discussion Points
1.   4.
2.   5.
3.   6.

Conclusion

Action items	[Presenter]
[Topic here]	[Name]
[Topic here]	[Name]
Any notes	

MEETING MINUTES TEMPLATE

Meeting Date:	
Meeting Time:	
Meeting Location:	
Meeting Called By: Designation:	
Meeting Purpose:	
Note Taker:	
Timekeeper:	

AGENDA TOPICS

[Write topic here]	[Presenter]
[Add another topic if any]	[Presenter]

Important Discussion Points
1.   4.
2.   5.
3.   6.

Conclusion

Action items	[Presenter]
[Topic here]	[Name]
[Topic here]	[Name]

Any notes

MEETING MINUTES TEMPLATE

Meeting Date:	
Meeting Time:	
Meeting Location:	
Meeting Called By:	Designation:
Meeting Purpose:	
Note Taker:	
Timekeeper:	

AGENDA TOPICS

[Write topic here]	[Presenter]
[Add another topic if any]	[Presenter]

Important Discussion Points
1.   4.
2.   5.
3.   6.

Conclusion

Action items	[Presenter]
[Topic here]	[Name]
[Topic here]	[Name]
Any notes	

MEETING MINUTES TEMPLATE

Meeting Date:	
Meeting Time:	
Meeting Location:	
Meeting Called By:	Designation:
Meeting Purpose:	
Note Taker:	
Timekeeper:	

AGENDA TOPICS

[Write topic here]	[Presenter]
[Add another topic if any]	[Presenter]

Important Discussion Points
1.   4.
2.   5.
3.   6.

Conclusion

Action items	[Presenter]
[Topic here]	[Name]
[Topic here]	[Name]
Any notes	

MEETING MINUTES TEMPLATE

Meeting Date:	
Meeting Time:	
Meeting Location:	
Meeting Called By: Designation:	
Meeting Purpose:	
Note Taker:	
Timekeeper:	

AGENDA TOPICS

[Write topic here]	[Presenter]
[Add another topic if any]	[Presenter]

Important Discussion Points
1. 4.
2. 5.
3. 6.

Conclusion

Action items	[Presenter]
[Topic here]	[Name]
[Topic here]	[Name]
Any notes	

MEETING MINUTES TEMPLATE

Meeting Date:	
Meeting Time:	
Meeting Location:	
Meeting Called By: Designation:	
Meeting Purpose:	
Note Taker:	
Timekeeper:	

AGENDA TOPICS

[Write topic here]	[Presenter]
[Add another topic if any]	[Presenter]

Important Discussion Points
1.   4.
2.   5.
3.   6.

Conclusion

Action items	[Presenter]
[Topic here]	[Name]
[Topic here]	[Name]

Any notes

MEETING MINUTES TEMPLATE

Meeting Date:	
Meeting Time:	
Meeting Location:	
Meeting Called By: Designation:	
Meeting Purpose:	
Note Taker:	
Timekeeper:	

AGENDA TOPICS

[Write topic here]	[Presenter]
[Add another topic if any]	[Presenter]

Important Discussion Points
1.   4.
2.   5.
3.   6.

Conclusion

Action items	[Presenter]
[Topic here]	[Name]
[Topic here]	[Name]
Any notes	

MEETING MINUTES TEMPLATE

Meeting Date:	
Meeting Time:	
Meeting Location:	
Meeting Called By:	Designation:
Meeting Purpose:	
Note Taker:	
Timekeeper:	

AGENDA TOPICS

[Write topic here]	[Presenter]
[Add another topic if any]	[Presenter]

Important Discussion Points	
1. 2. 3.	4. 5. 6.

Conclusion

Action items	[Presenter]
[Topic here]	[Name]
[Topic here]	[Name]
Any notes	

MEETING MINUTES TEMPLATE

Meeting Date:
Meeting Time:
Meeting Location:
Meeting Called By: Designation:
Meeting Purpose:
Note Taker:
Timekeeper:

AGENDA TOPICS

[Write topic here]	[Presenter]
[Add another topic if any]	[Presenter]

Important Discussion Points
1.   4.
2.   5.
3.   6.

Conclusion

Action items	[Presenter]
[Topic here]	[Name]
[Topic here]	[Name]
Any notes	

MEETING MINUTES TEMPLATE

Meeting Date:
Meeting Time:
Meeting Location:
Meeting Called By: Designation:
Meeting Purpose:
Note Taker:
Timekeeper:

AGENDA TOPICS

[Write topic here]	[Presenter]
[Add another topic if any]	[Presenter]

Important Discussion Points
1.   4.
2.   5.
3.   6.

Conclusion

Action items	[Presenter]
[Topic here]	[Name]
[Topic here]	[Name]
Any notes	

MEETING MINUTES TEMPLATE

Meeting Date:	
Meeting Time:	
Meeting Location:	
Meeting Called By: Designation:	
Meeting Purpose:	
Note Taker:	
Timekeeper:	

AGENDA TOPICS

[Write topic here] [Presenter]

[Add another topic if any] [Presenter]

Important Discussion Points
1. 4.
2. 5.
3. 6.

Conclusion

Action items [Presenter]

[Topic here] [Name]

[Topic here] [Name]

Any notes

MEETING MINUTES TEMPLATE

Meeting Date:	
Meeting Time:	
Meeting Location:	
Meeting Called By: Designation:	
Meeting Purpose:	
Note Taker:	
Timekeeper:	

AGENDA TOPICS

[Write topic here]	[Presenter]
[Add another topic if any]	[Presenter]

Important Discussion Points
1.   4.
2.   5.
3.   6.

Conclusion

Action items	[Presenter]
[Topic here]	[Name]
[Topic here]	[Name]

Any notes

MEETING MINUTES TEMPLATE

Meeting Date:
Meeting Time:
Meeting Location:
Meeting Called By: Designation:
Meeting Purpose:
Note Taker:
Timekeeper:

AGENDA TOPICS

[Write topic here]	[Presenter]
[Add another topic if any]	[Presenter]

Important Discussion Points
1.   4.
2.   5.
3.   6.

Conclusion

Action items	[Presenter]
[Topic here]	[Name]
[Topic here]	[Name]
Any notes	

MEETING MINUTES TEMPLATE

Meeting Date:	
Meeting Time:	
Meeting Location:	
Meeting Called By:	Designation:
Meeting Purpose:	
Note Taker:	
Timekeeper:	

AGENDA TOPICS

[Write topic here]	[Presenter]
[Add another topic if any]	[Presenter]

Important Discussion Points
1.   4.
2.   5.
3.   6.

Conclusion

Action items	[Presenter]
[Topic here]	[Name]
[Topic here]	[Name]
Any notes	

MEETING MINUTES TEMPLATE

Meeting Date:	
Meeting Time:	
Meeting Location:	
Meeting Called By: Designation:	
Meeting Purpose:	
Note Taker:	
Timekeeper:	

AGENDA TOPICS

[Write topic here]	[Presenter]
[Add another topic if any]	[Presenter]

Important Discussion Points
1. 4.
2. 5.
3. 6.

Conclusion

Action items	[Presenter]
[Topic here]	[Name]
[Topic here]	[Name]

Any notes

MEETING MINUTES TEMPLATE

Meeting Date:	
Meeting Time:	
Meeting Location:	
Meeting Called By:	Designation:
Meeting Purpose:	
Note Taker:	
Timekeeper:	

AGENDA TOPICS

[Write topic here]	[Presenter]
[Add another topic if any]	[Presenter]

Important Discussion Points
1.   4.
2.   5.
3.   6.

Conclusion

Action items	[Presenter]
[Topic here]	[Name]
[Topic here]	[Name]
Any notes	

MEETING MINUTES TEMPLATE

Meeting Date:	
Meeting Time:	
Meeting Location:	
Meeting Called By:	Designation:
Meeting Purpose:	
Note Taker:	
Timekeeper:	

AGENDA TOPICS

[Write topic here]	[Presenter]
[Add another topic if any]	[Presenter]

Important Discussion Points
1.   4.
2.   5.
3.   6.

Conclusion

Action items	[Presenter]
[Topic here]	[Name]
[Topic here]	[Name]
Any notes	

MEETING MINUTES TEMPLATE

Meeting Date:	
Meeting Time:	
Meeting Location:	
Meeting Called By: Designation:	
Meeting Purpose:	
Note Taker:	
Timekeeper:	

AGENDA TOPICS

[Write topic here]	[Presenter]
[Add another topic if any]	[Presenter]

Important Discussion Points
1. 4.
2. 5.
3. 6.

Conclusion

Action items	[Presenter]
[Topic here]	[Name]
[Topic here]	[Name]

Any notes

MEETING MINUTES TEMPLATE

Meeting Date:	
Meeting Time:	
Meeting Location:	
Meeting Called By:	Designation:
Meeting Purpose:	
Note Taker:	
Timekeeper:	

AGENDA TOPICS

[Write topic here]	[Presenter]
[Add another topic if any]	[Presenter]

Important Discussion Points
1. 4.
2. 5.
3. 6.

Conclusion

Action items	[Presenter]
[Topic here]	[Name]
[Topic here]	[Name]
Any notes	

MEETING MINUTES TEMPLATE

Meeting Date:
Meeting Time:
Meeting Location:
Meeting Called By: Designation:
Meeting Purpose:
Note Taker:
Timekeeper:

AGENDA TOPICS

[Write topic here]	[Presenter]
[Add another topic if any]	[Presenter]

Important Discussion Points

1.   4.
2.   5.
3.   6.

Conclusion

Action items	[Presenter]
[Topic here]	[Name]
[Topic here]	[Name]

Any notes

MEETING MINUTES TEMPLATE

Meeting Date:	
Meeting Time:	
Meeting Location:	
Meeting Called By: Designation:	
Meeting Purpose:	
Note Taker:	
Timekeeper:	

AGENDA TOPICS

[Write topic here]	[Presenter]
[Add another topic if any]	[Presenter]

Important Discussion Points
1. 4.
2. 5.
3. 6.

Conclusion

Action items	[Presenter]
[Topic here]	[Name]
[Topic here]	[Name]
Any notes	

MEETING MINUTES TEMPLATE

Meeting Date:	
Meeting Time:	
Meeting Location:	
Meeting Called By:	Designation:
Meeting Purpose:	
Note Taker:	
Timekeeper:	

AGENDA TOPICS

[Write topic here]	[Presenter]
[Add another topic if any]	[Presenter]

Important Discussion Points
1.   4.
2.   5.
3.   6.

Conclusion

Action items	[Presenter]
[Topic here]	[Name]
[Topic here]	[Name]
Any notes	

MEETING MINUTES TEMPLATE

Meeting Date:	
Meeting Time:	
Meeting Location:	
Meeting Called By:	Designation:
Meeting Purpose:	
Note Taker:	
Timekeeper:	

AGENDA TOPICS

[Write topic here]	[Presenter]
[Add another topic if any]	[Presenter]

Important Discussion Points
1.   4.
2.   5.
3.   6.

Conclusion

Action items	[Presenter]
[Topic here]	[Name]
[Topic here]	[Name]

Any notes

MEETING MINUTES TEMPLATE

Meeting Date:	
Meeting Time:	
Meeting Location:	
Meeting Called By: Designation:	
Meeting Purpose:	
Note Taker:	
Timekeeper:	

AGENDA TOPICS

[Write topic here]	[Presenter]
[Add another topic if any]	[Presenter]

Important Discussion Points

1.   4.
2.   5.
3.   6.

Conclusion

Action items	[Presenter]
[Topic here]	[Name]
[Topic here]	[Name]
Any notes	

MEETING MINUTES TEMPLATE

Meeting Date:	
Meeting Time:	
Meeting Location:	
Meeting Called By:	Designation:
Meeting Purpose:	
Note Taker:	
Timekeeper:	

AGENDA TOPICS

[Write topic here]	[Presenter]
[Add another topic if any]	[Presenter]

Important Discussion Points
1. 4.
2. 5.
3. 6.

Conclusion

Action items	[Presenter]
[Topic here]	[Name]
[Topic here]	[Name]
Any notes	

MEETING MINUTES TEMPLATE

Meeting Date:	
Meeting Time:	
Meeting Location:	
Meeting Called By:	Designation:
Meeting Purpose:	
Note Taker:	
Timekeeper:	

AGENDA TOPICS

[Write topic here]	[Presenter]
[Add another topic if any]	[Presenter]

Important Discussion Points
1.   4.
2.   5.
3.   6.

Conclusion

Action items	[Presenter]
[Topic here]	[Name]
[Topic here]	[Name]
Any notes	

MEETING MINUTES TEMPLATE

Meeting Date:	
Meeting Time:	
Meeting Location:	
Meeting Called By:	Designation:
Meeting Purpose:	
Note Taker:	
Timekeeper:	

AGENDA TOPICS

[Write topic here]	[Presenter]
[Add another topic if any]	[Presenter]

Important Discussion Points
1.   4.
2.   5.
3.   6.

Conclusion

Action items	[Presenter]
[Topic here]	[Name]
[Topic here]	[Name]
Any notes	

MEETING MINUTES TEMPLATE

Meeting Date:	
Meeting Time:	
Meeting Location:	
Meeting Called By:	Designation:
Meeting Purpose:	
Note Taker:	
Timekeeper:	

AGENDA TOPICS

[Write topic here]	[Presenter]
[Add another topic if any]	[Presenter]

Important Discussion Points

1. 4.
2. 5.
3. 6.

Conclusion

Action items	[Presenter]
[Topic here]	[Name]
[Topic here]	[Name]

Any notes

MEETING MINUTES TEMPLATE

Meeting Date:	
Meeting Time:	
Meeting Location:	
Meeting Called By:	Designation:
Meeting Purpose:	
Note Taker:	
Timekeeper:	

AGENDA TOPICS

[Write topic here]	[Presenter]
[Add another topic if any]	[Presenter]

Important Discussion Points

1.   4.
2.   5.
3.   6.

Conclusion

Action items	[Presenter]
[Topic here]	[Name]
[Topic here]	[Name]
Any notes	

MEETING MINUTES TEMPLATE

Meeting Date:	
Meeting Time:	
Meeting Location:	
Meeting Called By: Designation:	
Meeting Purpose:	
Note Taker:	
Timekeeper:	

AGENDA TOPICS

[Write topic here]	[Presenter]
[Add another topic if any]	[Presenter]

Important Discussion Points

1.   4.
2.   5.
3.   6.

Conclusion

Action items	[Presenter]
[Topic here]	[Name]
[Topic here]	[Name]
Any notes	

MEETING MINUTES TEMPLATE

Meeting Date:	
Meeting Time:	
Meeting Location:	
Meeting Called By:	Designation:
Meeting Purpose:	
Note Taker:	
Timekeeper:	

AGENDA TOPICS

[Write topic here]	[Presenter]
[Add another topic if any]	[Presenter]

Important Discussion Points

1.   4.
2.   5.
3.   6.

Conclusion

Action items	[Presenter]
[Topic here]	[Name]
[Topic here]	[Name]
Any notes	

MEETING MINUTES TEMPLATE

Meeting Date:	
Meeting Time:	
Meeting Location:	
Meeting Called By:	Designation:
Meeting Purpose:	
Note Taker:	
Timekeeper:	

AGENDA TOPICS

[Write topic here]	[Presenter]
[Add another topic if any]	[Presenter]

Important Discussion Points
1.   4.
2.   5.
3.   6.

Conclusion

Action items	[Presenter]
[Topic here]	[Name]
[Topic here]	[Name]
Any notes	

MEETING MINUTES TEMPLATE

Meeting Date:	
Meeting Time:	
Meeting Location:	
Meeting Called By: Designation:	
Meeting Purpose:	
Note Taker:	
Timekeeper:	

AGENDA TOPICS

[Write topic here]	[Presenter]
[Add another topic if any]	[Presenter]

Important Discussion Points
1.   4.
2.   5.
3.   6.

Conclusion

Action items	[Presenter]
[Topic here]	[Name]
[Topic here]	[Name]
Any notes	

MEETING MINUTES TEMPLATE

Meeting Date:
Meeting Time:
Meeting Location:
Meeting Called By: Designation:
Meeting Purpose:
Note Taker:
Timekeeper:

AGENDA TOPICS

[Write topic here]	[Presenter]
[Add another topic if any]	[Presenter]

Important Discussion Points
1.   4.
2.   5.
3.   6.

Conclusion

Action items	[Presenter]
[Topic here]	[Name]
[Topic here]	[Name]

Any notes

MEETING MINUTES TEMPLATE

Meeting Date:	
Meeting Time:	
Meeting Location:	
Meeting Called By:	Designation:
Meeting Purpose:	
Note Taker:	
Timekeeper:	

AGENDA TOPICS

[Write topic here]   [Presenter]

[Add another topic if any]   [Presenter]

Important Discussion Points
1.   4.
2.   5.
3.   6.

Conclusion

Action items   [Presenter]

[Topic here]   [Name]

[Topic here]   [Name]

Any notes

MEETING MINUTES TEMPLATE

Meeting Date:	
Meeting Time:	
Meeting Location:	
Meeting Called By: Designation:	
Meeting Purpose:	
Note Taker:	
Timekeeper:	

AGENDA TOPICS

[Write topic here]	[Presenter]
[Add another topic if any]	[Presenter]

Important Discussion Points	
1.	4.
2.	5.
3.	6.

Conclusion

Action items	[Presenter]
[Topic here]	[Name]
[Topic here]	[Name]
Any notes	

MEETING MINUTES TEMPLATE

Meeting Date:	
Meeting Time:	
Meeting Location:	
Meeting Called By:	Designation:
Meeting Purpose:	
Note Taker:	
Timekeeper:	

AGENDA TOPICS

[Write topic here]	[Presenter]
[Add another topic if any]	[Presenter]

Important Discussion Points
1.   4.
2.   5.
3.   6.

Conclusion

Action items	[Presenter]
[Topic here]	[Name]
[Topic here]	[Name]
Any notes	

MEETING MINUTES TEMPLATE

Meeting Date:	
Meeting Time:	
Meeting Location:	
Meeting Called By: Designation:	
Meeting Purpose:	
Note Taker:	
Timekeeper:	

AGENDA TOPICS

[Write topic here]	[Presenter]
[Add another topic if any]	[Presenter]

Important Discussion Points
1.   4.
2.   5.
3.   6.

Conclusion

Action items	[Presenter]
[Topic here]	[Name]
[Topic here]	[Name]

Any notes

MEETING MINUTES TEMPLATE

Meeting Date:	
Meeting Time:	
Meeting Location:	
Meeting Called By:	Designation:
Meeting Purpose:	
Note Taker:	
Timekeeper:	

AGENDA TOPICS

[Write topic here]	[Presenter]
[Add another topic if any]	[Presenter]

Important Discussion Points
1.   4.
2.   5.
3.   6.

Conclusion

Action items	[Presenter]
[Topic here]	[Name]
[Topic here]	[Name]
Any notes	

MEETING MINUTES TEMPLATE

Meeting Date:	
Meeting Time:	
Meeting Location:	
Meeting Called By:	Designation:
Meeting Purpose:	
Note Taker:	
Timekeeper:	

AGENDA TOPICS

[Write topic here]	[Presenter]
[Add another topic if any]	[Presenter]

Important Discussion Points	
1.	4.
2.	5.
3.	6.

Conclusion

Action items	[Presenter]
[Topic here]	[Name]
[Topic here]	[Name]
Any notes	

MEETING MINUTES TEMPLATE

Meeting Date:	
Meeting Time:	
Meeting Location:	
Meeting Called By: Designation:	
Meeting Purpose:	
Note Taker:	
Timekeeper:	

AGENDA TOPICS

[Write topic here]	[Presenter]
[Add another topic if any]	[Presenter]

Important Discussion Points
1.   4.
2.   5.
3.   6.

Conclusion

Action items	[Presenter]
[Topic here]	[Name]
[Topic here]	[Name]
Any notes	

MEETING MINUTES TEMPLATE

Meeting Date:
Meeting Time:
Meeting Location:
Meeting Called By: Designation:
Meeting Purpose:
Note Taker:
Timekeeper:

AGENDA TOPICS

[Write topic here]	[Presenter]
[Add another topic if any]	[Presenter]

Important Discussion Points
1.   4.
2.   5.
3.   6.

Conclusion

Action items	[Presenter]
[Topic here]	[Name]
[Topic here]	[Name]
Any notes	

MEETING MINUTES TEMPLATE

Meeting Date:	
Meeting Time:	
Meeting Location:	
Meeting Called By: Designation:	
Meeting Purpose:	
Note Taker:	
Timekeeper:	

AGENDA TOPICS

[Write topic here]	[Presenter]
[Add another topic if any]	[Presenter]

Important Discussion Points
1. 4.
2. 5.
3. 6.

Conclusion

Action items	[Presenter]
[Topic here]	[Name]
[Topic here]	[Name]

Any notes

MEETING MINUTES TEMPLATE

Meeting Date:	
Meeting Time:	
Meeting Location:	
Meeting Called By: Designation:	
Meeting Purpose:	
Note Taker:	
Timekeeper:	

AGENDA TOPICS

[Write topic here]	[Presenter]
[Add another topic if any]	[Presenter]

Important Discussion Points
1.   4.
2.   5.
3.   6.

Conclusion

Action items	[Presenter]
[Topic here]	[Name]
[Topic here]	[Name]
Any notes	

MEETING MINUTES TEMPLATE

Meeting Date:	
Meeting Time:	
Meeting Location:	
Meeting Called By: Designation:	
Meeting Purpose:	
Note Taker:	
Timekeeper:	

AGENDA TOPICS

[Write topic here]	[Presenter]
[Add another topic if any]	[Presenter]

Important Discussion Points
1.   4.
2.   5.
3.   6.

Conclusion

Action items	[Presenter]
[Topic here]	[Name]
[Topic here]	[Name]
Any notes	

MEETING MINUTES TEMPLATE

Meeting Date:	
Meeting Time:	
Meeting Location:	
Meeting Called By:	Designation:
Meeting Purpose:	
Note Taker:	
Timekeeper:	

AGENDA TOPICS

[Write topic here]	[Presenter]
[Add another topic if any]	[Presenter]

Important Discussion Points
1. 4.
2. 5.
3. 6.

Conclusion

Action items	[Presenter]
[Topic here]	[Name]
[Topic here]	[Name]

Any notes

MEETING MINUTES TEMPLATE

Meeting Date:	
Meeting Time:	
Meeting Location:	
Meeting Called By: Designation:	
Meeting Purpose:	
Note Taker:	
Timekeeper:	

AGENDA TOPICS

[Write topic here]	[Presenter]
[Add another topic if any]	[Presenter]

Important Discussion Points
1.   4.
2.   5.
3.   6.

Conclusion

Action items	[Presenter]
[Topic here]	[Name]
[Topic here]	[Name]
Any notes	

MEETING MINUTES TEMPLATE

Meeting Date:
Meeting Time:
Meeting Location:
Meeting Called By: Designation:
Meeting Purpose:
Note Taker:
Timekeeper:

AGENDA TOPICS

[Write topic here]	[Presenter]
[Add another topic if any]	[Presenter]

Important Discussion Points
1.   4.
2.   5.
3.   6.
Conclusion

Action items	[Presenter]
[Topic here]	[Name]
[Topic here]	[Name]
Any notes	

MEETING MINUTES TEMPLATE

Meeting Date:	
Meeting Time:	
Meeting Location:	
Meeting Called By:	Designation:
Meeting Purpose:	
Note Taker:	
Timekeeper:	

AGENDA TOPICS

[Write topic here]	[Presenter]
[Add another topic if any]	[Presenter]

Important Discussion Points
1.   4.
2.   5.
3.   6.

Conclusion

Action items	[Presenter]
[Topic here]	[Name]
[Topic here]	[Name]
Any notes	

MEETING MINUTES TEMPLATE

Meeting Date:	
Meeting Time:	
Meeting Location:	
Meeting Called By: Designation:	
Meeting Purpose:	
Note Taker:	
Timekeeper:	

AGENDA TOPICS

[Write topic here]	[Presenter]
[Add another topic if any]	[Presenter]

Important Discussion Points
1.   4.
2.   5.
3.   6.

Conclusion

Action items	[Presenter]
[Topic here]	[Name]
[Topic here]	[Name]

Any notes

MEETING MINUTES TEMPLATE

Meeting Date:	
Meeting Time:	
Meeting Location:	
Meeting Called By:	Designation:
Meeting Purpose:	
Note Taker:	
Timekeeper:	

AGENDA TOPICS

[Write topic here]	[Presenter]
[Add another topic if any]	[Presenter]

Important Discussion Points

1.   4.
2.   5.
3.   6.

Conclusion

Action items	[Presenter]
[Topic here]	[Name]
[Topic here]	[Name]
Any notes	

MEETING MINUTES TEMPLATE

Meeting Date:
Meeting Time:
Meeting Location:
Meeting Called By: Designation:
Meeting Purpose:
Note Taker:
Timekeeper:

AGENDA TOPICS

[Write topic here]	[Presenter]
[Add another topic if any]	[Presenter]

Important Discussion Points	
1.	4.
2.	5.
3.	6.

Conclusion

Action items	[Presenter]
[Topic here]	[Name]
[Topic here]	[Name]
Any notes	

MEETING MINUTES TEMPLATE

Meeting Date:	
Meeting Time:	
Meeting Location:	
Meeting Called By: Designation:	
Meeting Purpose:	
Note Taker:	
Timekeeper:	

AGENDA TOPICS

[Write topic here]	[Presenter]
[Add another topic if any]	[Presenter]

Important Discussion Points
1.   4.
2.   5.
3.   6.

Conclusion

Action items	[Presenter]
[Topic here]	[Name]
[Topic here]	[Name]
Any notes	

MEETING MINUTES TEMPLATE

Meeting Date:	
Meeting Time:	
Meeting Location:	
Meeting Called By:	Designation:
Meeting Purpose:	
Note Taker:	
Timekeeper:	

AGENDA TOPICS

[Write topic here]	[Presenter]
[Add another topic if any]	[Presenter]

Important Discussion Points

1.   4.
2.   5.
3.   6.

Conclusion

Action items	[Presenter]
[Topic here]	[Name]
[Topic here]	[Name]
Any notes	

MEETING MINUTES TEMPLATE

Meeting Date:	
Meeting Time:	
Meeting Location:	
Meeting Called By:	Designation:
Meeting Purpose:	
Note Taker:	
Timekeeper:	

AGENDA TOPICS

[Write topic here]	[Presenter]
[Add another topic if any]	[Presenter]

Important Discussion Points
1. 4.
2. 5.
3. 6.

Conclusion

Action items	[Presenter]
[Topic here]	[Name]
[Topic here]	[Name]
Any notes	

MEETING MINUTES TEMPLATE

Meeting Date:	
Meeting Time:	
Meeting Location:	
Meeting Called By:	Designation:
Meeting Purpose:	
Note Taker:	
Timekeeper:	

AGENDA TOPICS

[Write topic here]	[Presenter]
[Add another topic if any]	[Presenter]

Important Discussion Points
1.   4.
2.   5.
3.   6.

Conclusion

Action items	[Presenter]
[Topic here]	[Name]
[Topic here]	[Name]

Any notes

MEETING MINUTES TEMPLATE

Meeting Date:	
Meeting Time:	
Meeting Location:	
Meeting Called By: Designation:	
Meeting Purpose:	
Note Taker:	
Timekeeper:	

AGENDA TOPICS

[Write topic here]	[Presenter]
[Add another topic if any]	[Presenter]

Important Discussion Points	
1.	4.
2.	5.
3.	6.

Conclusion

Action items	[Presenter]
[Topic here]	[Name]
[Topic here]	[Name]
Any notes	

MEETING MINUTES TEMPLATE

Meeting Date:	
Meeting Time:	
Meeting Location:	
Meeting Called By: Designation:	
Meeting Purpose:	
Note Taker:	
Timekeeper:	

AGENDA TOPICS

[Write topic here]	[Presenter]
[Add another topic if any]	[Presenter]

Important Discussion Points
1.   4.
2.   5.
3.   6.

Conclusion

Action items	[Presenter]
[Topic here]	[Name]
[Topic here]	[Name]
Any notes	

MEETING MINUTES TEMPLATE

Meeting Date:	
Meeting Time:	
Meeting Location:	
Meeting Called By:	Designation:
Meeting Purpose:	
Note Taker:	
Timekeeper:	

AGENDA TOPICS

[Write topic here]	[Presenter]
[Add another topic if any]	[Presenter]

Important Discussion Points
1.   4.
2.   5.
3.   6.

Conclusion

Action items	[Presenter]
[Topic here]	[Name]
[Topic here]	[Name]
Any notes	

MEETING MINUTES TEMPLATE

Meeting Date:	
Meeting Time:	
Meeting Location:	
Meeting Called By:	Designation:
Meeting Purpose:	
Note Taker:	
Timekeeper:	

AGENDA TOPICS

[Write topic here]	[Presenter]
[Add another topic if any]	[Presenter]

Important Discussion Points
1.   4.
2.   5.
3.   6.

Conclusion

Action items	[Presenter]
[Topic here]	[Name]
[Topic here]	[Name]

Any notes

MEETING MINUTES TEMPLATE

Meeting Date:	
Meeting Time:	
Meeting Location:	
Meeting Called By:	Designation:
Meeting Purpose:	
Note Taker:	
Timekeeper:	

AGENDA TOPICS

[Write topic here]	[Presenter]
[Add another topic if any]	[Presenter]

Important Discussion Points
1.   4.
2.   5.
3.   6.

Conclusion

Action items	[Presenter]
[Topic here]	[Name]
[Topic here]	[Name]
Any notes	

MEETING MINUTES TEMPLATE

Meeting Date:	
Meeting Time:	
Meeting Location:	
Meeting Called By:	Designation:
Meeting Purpose:	
Note Taker:	
Timekeeper:	

AGENDA TOPICS

[Write topic here]	[Presenter]
[Add another topic if any]	[Presenter]

Important Discussion Points
1.   4.
2.   5.
3.   6.

Conclusion

Action items	[Presenter]
[Topic here]	[Name]
[Topic here]	[Name]
Any notes	

MEETING MINUTES TEMPLATE

Meeting Date:	
Meeting Time:	
Meeting Location:	
Meeting Called By:	Designation:
Meeting Purpose:	
Note Taker:	
Timekeeper:	

AGENDA TOPICS

[Write topic here]	[Presenter]
[Add another topic if any]	[Presenter]

Important Discussion Points
1. 4.
2. 5.
3. 6.

Conclusion

Action items	[Presenter]
[Topic here]	[Name]
[Topic here]	[Name]
Any notes	

MEETING MINUTES TEMPLATE

Meeting Date:	
Meeting Time:	
Meeting Location:	
Meeting Called By:	Designation:
Meeting Purpose:	
Note Taker:	
Timekeeper:	

AGENDA TOPICS

[Write topic here]	[Presenter]
[Add another topic if any]	[Presenter]

Important Discussion Points
1.
2.
3.
4.
5.
6.

Conclusion

Action items	[Presenter]
[Topic here]	[Name]
[Topic here]	[Name]

Any notes

MEETING MINUTES TEMPLATE

Meeting Date:	
Meeting Time:	
Meeting Location:	
Meeting Called By:	Designation:
Meeting Purpose:	
Note Taker:	
Timekeeper:	

AGENDA TOPICS

[Write topic here]	[Presenter]
[Add another topic if any]	[Presenter]

Important Discussion Points
1.   4.
2.   5.
3.   6.

Conclusion

Action items	[Presenter]
[Topic here]	[Name]
[Topic here]	[Name]

Any notes

MEETING MINUTES TEMPLATE

Meeting Date:	
Meeting Time:	
Meeting Location:	
Meeting Called By: Designation:	
Meeting Purpose:	
Note Taker:	
Timekeeper:	

AGENDA TOPICS

[Write topic here]	[Presenter]
[Add another topic if any]	[Presenter]

Important Discussion Points

1.   4.
2.   5.
3.   6.

Conclusion

Action items	[Presenter]
[Topic here]	[Name]
[Topic here]	[Name]

Any notes